The
Winologist

Aaron Shawn Harper

Aaron Shawn Harper

Copyright © 2022 by Aaron Shawn Harper. All rights reserved.
No part of this publication may be reproduced, stored in a retrieval system, or transmitted in any form or by any means, electronic, mechanical, photocopying, recording, scanning, or otherwise, except as permitted under Section 107 or 108 of the 1976 United States Copyright Act, without either the prior written permission of the Publisher, or authorization through payment of the appropriate per-copy fee to the Copyright Clearance Center, Inc., 222 Rosewood Drive, Danvers, MA 01923, (978) 750-8400, fax (978) 646-8600, or on the web at www.copyright.com
ISBN:

CONTENTS

PREFACE	4
THE START	5
THE WEIGHT OF REJECTION	13
DISCIPLINE	23
WINNING STRATEGIES	33
UNDERSTANDING YOURSELF	51
UNDERSTANDING HINDRANCES	58
WALKING THROUGH FORGIVENESS	71
LIVING A LIFE FILLED WITH GRATITUDE	78

Preface

I became "The Winologist" by spending a significant amount of time studying the lives and habits of winners. I also learned a lot about winning in my own life by failing. To conquer anything, you should understand that in the process, you may fall flat on your face, but you can still get back up and seize your victory!

The man I am today is far from what I expected or envisioned as a young boy. By God's foreknowledge and abundant grace, along with hard work and determination, the challenges of my childhood became the springboard for making a profound impact on the lives of hundreds of thousands of people!

Many may know my name, but not my full story. I hope that by the time you reach the final page of this book, you are convinced that regardless of the playing field you were handed in life or how you started the game, it's the *way* you play that will determine if or how you win!

The Start

"You can't always control circumstances. However, you can always control your attitude, approach, and response. Your options are to complain or to look ahead and figure out how to make the situation better." — Tony Dungy, Head coach, Tampa Bay Buccaneers (1996-2001), Indianapolis Colts (2002-08)

I was born with more potential than many would believe or say about me. I'm certain that my parents experienced joy and hope with my birth, but I think that it may have been short-lived.

The 1970's decade in the United States was filled with soaring inflation and political upheaval. For families like mine that were barely above the poverty line, this caused additional stress on my parents. Unfortunately, their responses at times involved unnecessary emotional abuse.

When I was little, my father was a manager at the local Pizza Hut and would often bring home an assortment of pizza pies. While this might sound like every kid's dream, there is only a certain amount of the same food that a person can eat before growing tired of it.

My siblings would often take leftover slices to school to barter with other students for things we never got. I would often refuse the pizza my father offered because they contained anchovies that I just could not stomach. He would become enraged by my unwillingness to eat the pizza he brought home to feed me.

I remember him sitting me down to discipline me. His voice carried so much authority that it was impossible to feel unmoved by it. Words do carry weight, and it's often not what is said but *how* it is said that makes the greater impact.

Much of what my father said repeats itself like a prayer. As an adult, I understand now that what he said and did to me as a child was all he knew. Our parents often parent us the way they were brought up. Sometimes that means we will end up with blood on our hands from wounds in their lives that were caused long ago.

That is what my father did. He bled on people who had not cut him. It takes a lot of maturity to recognize that our parents handled us the best way they knew at the time.

I remember him picking me up and tossing me down the stairs over and over. I found myself standing back up and returning to him with outstretched arms, aching for him to see me as a son.

I wanted him to see me and love me. I thought that if I returned to him sorrowfully and whispered "*I love you,*" he would be reminded of his fatherly duties and love me.

This is not what happened. It was a painful experience. I finally realized that my father did not have the capability to love me the way a child needs, and our relationship was void of trust and filled with rejection.

By definition, rejection is dismissal or refusal of a person, a behavior, beliefs, or ideas. Growing up, I experienced a dismissal from my father that felt like I was not worthy of love.

In one abusive episode, my brother stepped in and hid me in the garage until my mother came home. I was scared of what might come yet hopeful that my mother would address my father and stop the abuse. Within a year of that turmoil, my father and mother divorced.

At the time, my father held a lot of power as a preacher and associate in one of the most prominent African American churches in Columbus. He had succumbed to an illicit affair and left. This is a confession that most children would not hear from their parents, so the children end up in therapy trying to piece together a life that was never supposed to be broken.

My mother was left raising six children. I watched as she would take on several jobs to ensure we kept a roof over our heads and food in our bellies. She would take the bus to the wealthier parts of Columbus to work as a maid, scrubbing floors and cleaning up other people's messes.

I found it ironic that she was cleaning up their homes while the mess at our home, with my father, left us in disarray. However, regardless of the kind of day my mother had, she would always come home with a smile and share stories. Simmering underneath, though, was pain that no one could relieve her from; at a certain point, she attempted to take her own life.

Poverty is expensive. It deprives you of more than just materials. It takes away valuable family time. Many low-income households have mothers raising other people's kids while their own kids sit at home trying to parent themselves.

My siblings had to raise me as my mother worked. As much as I loved my siblings, I would have loved to know a soft mother's touch and the firm, guiding hand of a father.

Usually, kids who have a difficult home life find some comfort in school. It provides eight to ten hours away from the chaos, but there was no escape from hurt and rejection for me. School was challenging for me; I faced many hills that turned into mountains.

I had to repeat the first grade. I remember being in the first grade and seeing the friends I had the previous year in a different class. They wanted nothing to do with me as they saw me as stupid for staying behind another year.

I never realized the pain that I would experience. I was coming from an unstable home, only to escape to an institution where I felt more unwelcome, clinging to the ache of never being enough.

I was reading at a kindergarten level while my peers excelled. Despite repeating the first grade, I still struggled. I felt that placing me back in the same grade did absolutely nothing.

To make matters worse, I was bullied. Despite the decades that have passed since my early years of schooling, I still remember being called specific names. I was called *Crud McMud* as I played in the mud, being constantly dirty and having dump trucks for toys. I was also called *BB and Boy Scout* because my hair was nappy all the time. These were just words to the kids, but they became daggers to my self-esteem.

As my older brothers left the home, my household became predominantly female. My mother was worried that I did not have enough male influence. So, when I was in the third grade, she encouraged me to join the football team to be around "men" that would help me to grow in character and develop masculinity.

I would walk a mile and a half each way to play football, but I was dreadful at it. Back then, all football teams were picked according to weight category. As a heavy kid, I was placed with the fifth graders when I was only in second grade, so I experienced additional bullying and wrath. I had no safe space to be myself or focus my efforts to become the best version of myself.

It was incredibly lonely and depressing being a boy in a world that did not want me. I was trying to navigate through a life that did not want to offer me any directions.

Hurt(ing) people, hurt people. Bullying does one of two things to people; they either relinquish all power and become a submissive puppet to the bullies, or they savor power and become the bully.

I chose the latter. I internalized the hate I experienced and started spitting it out to those around me. How others treat us impacts the way we see and portray ourselves.

In the fifth grade, I had a teacher who empathized with me and asked me to be tested for learning disabilities. It resulted in a diagnosis of five different learning disabilities. They recommended that I join special learning classes, which at the time had many negative names attached to them. My mother fought against it.

For better or for worse, she did not want me to be attached to a degrading image, so she put me back in the regular classes. It was excruciating to be without any accommodations.

I remember the pain I felt when I had to spell things on the board or calculate simple mathematical sums. Back then, no one cared about holding back laughs and taunts that students directed at their peers. I felt like a walking joke. Fifth grade was tough, and it replays like a broken record.

I also recall being ashamed of our poverty. We had to use food stamps and welfare to get by. Despite being shackled with these chains, God was there with us being good to us, as only He is.

Whenever my mother cried out to God, I would see a move in our life. I was in awe of her relationship with God. There was an undeniable covenant between her and God, and we all experienced the blessings of her obedience.

Although poor, we had the best house on our block, we had enough material things to live on, and we constantly experienced favor from others. It was unseen or unheard of that a family drenched in poverty could have their every need met. Neighbors even became suspicious of us. At one point, social service agencies were called in to investigate our spending.

In this season of hardship, poverty, abuse, and bullying, I learned important lessons by witnessing my mother's faith. I saw the spiritual law of finances combined with unshakeable belief.

No matter where you come from or who you are, God calls you by name *(Isa. 43:1)*, redeems you *(Isa. 52:7)*, establishes and strengthens you *(2 Cor. 1:21)*, sets you apart *(1 Pet. 2:9-10)*, has a purpose for you *(Jer. 29:11)*, and wants you to experience life in abundance *(2 Cor. 9:8)*, filled with blessings *(Eph. 1:3)* that glorify Him in all your works *(1 Pet. 4:10-11)*.

The Weight of Rejection

"Stay focused. Your start does not determine how you're going to finish." -- Herm Edwards, Head Coach New York Jets (2001-05), Kansas City Chiefs (2006-08)

Children first perceive the idea of love from their parents, but like I did, many children carry the weight of unhealed parents. These burdens have been passed down from generation to generation but were never dealt with and rectified. Then the children end up accepting this as part of who they are.

For as much hurt as I experienced as a child in my home, I do not blame my parents. I understand that my parents were emotionally immature. Emotional immaturity festers into emotional neglect, which leaves children in a volatile space.

As a child, I could not recognize this emotional neglect or rejection as a "their-problem" instead of a "me-problem". I wish that I could tell my ten-year-old self, drowning in rejection and loneliness, that there was nothing wrong with me. I wish I could tell that version of myself that it wasn't my fault that I received wrath instead of comfort for showing emotions that my parents were not secure enough to confront.

I learned to place my feelings in a box to deal with theirs. I would often carry a heavy heart back to my father, wanting him to empathize with me and love me, but my father was emotionally disconnected and it was difficult for him to have compassion for me.

This creates a huge psychological impact on the growing minds of children. As children begin to grow and see that there is no (helpful) response from their parents concerning the emotions they experience, the less likely they will share those feelings. These patterns of emotional neglect create feelings of rejection, which ultimately becomes a mindset.

Rejection does many things to people.
For some, it leaves them filled with burning rage, unwilling to enter any relationship that will require intimacy. Fear rules these individuals. They are constantly tormented with thoughts of not being enough or being unworthy, so they end relationships quickly.

Others feel vacant and constantly crave relationships. Sometimes these people take significant risks with their safety and health to "be enough" for someone so that they won't leave.

They are often left loving the *idea* of having a person rather than loving the person. Regardless of how rejected people decide to express themselves, there are deep roots of low self-esteem, chronic self-doubt, anxiety, and depression.

Rejection at School

As I mentioned before, I encountered many hardships in school. Bullying, insecurity in my identity, and feelings of rejection reigned in my life. In the 5th and 6th grades, I faced countless attacks from my peers on my character, appearance, and financial situation. I was also older than everyone in my class, adding to my low self-esteem.

In psychology, self-esteem is subjective. This means that the worth or value you feel or perceive may be a flawed perception of self that flows over into your relationships. People treat you the way you treat yourself. You set the foundations of how you expect others to love and treat you.

John C. Maxwell said, *"If you want others to treat you more kindly, you must develop better people skills. There is no sure way to make other people in your environment improve."* Because I had low self-esteem rising from the rejection I experienced, the lens through which I saw and experienced relationships was flawed.

Based on psychological studies, some children whose parents reject them often grow up expecting this same treatment from others. However, other children develop supernatural resilience in which hurt bounces off their hearts. They focus all their attention on being the best at their job or seeking high levels of achievement.

While this was not wholly my experience, I did want to feel and be included in certain groups and environments. We all have a choice. I had a choice. Would I choose to have rejection define me and see myself through the lens that others did? Or would I decide to push forward, heal, and become the best version of myself? I chose the latter, but that unfolded in time.

After experiencing so much hurt, rejection, and bullying in the fifth and sixth grades, I had little hope for the rest of my schooling. In the seventh grade, I was assaulted and jumped. By the eighth grade, I was involved in a major fight with a teacher, and I was expelled.

I started at a new school, feeling anxious about the possibility of being rejected by my peers once again. A few weeks later, I was expelled from that school and transferred to yet another.

I did not realize that this third school would prepare me for a success mindset. Mindset is important. I had allowed people, things, and environments to push me around and to dictate my identity.

I felt and thought *like* a failure. Do you see that I didn't say that I *was* a failure? Being in a bad season does not mean that you are a failure. It was always possible for me to get out of the hole I allowed people to push me into.

At this high school, I went to see a football coach who said that I could play. I was nonchalant; unable to believe and see the possibility of my success in football. I was unable to believe any good words spoken over me.

I was filled with so much unbelief in myself that it was difficult for me to even trust this coach who had a keen eye and could discern the capability in someone else. Coaches are equipped to see a diamond in the rough, but I had trouble believing him.

Regardless of how I felt, I showed up and trained. It was not too long before I was kicked off the team for disciplinary issues. As I sat inside the locker room, packing and preparing to leave, something rose up inside me. I was introduced to one of my best characteristics, tenacity. I refused to believe that something good that had become a part of my life would now be taken away from me.

I couldn't just quit. Subconsciously, I knew my coach saw something positive in me, and I refused to be handcuffed to the past to keep me from being liberated for my future.

I charged towards my coach on the practice field, who turned to me and yelled, "What do you want?!" I had my hands hung at my sides, balled into fists, and said, **"I will not quit!"** He, seeing that I was determined to do better for myself, yelled "Then get back in line!" He knew this was a defining moment in my life.

I constantly think back to this day, knowing that if I had let my past behaviors and mannerisms determine my future, I would not have a name today. I was a sub-par athlete with no accolades. This is almost unheard of in sports. Everyone receives at least one achievement when playing football, but I did not have even one.

Along with my learning disabilities, I was flat-footed. Some consider this to be a deformity. In the NFL, I visited several doctors overseas with the hopes of getting help.

I went to Johannesburg, South Africa, where the doctor who attended me was taken aback by my flat feet. He was using high-tech equipment and was stunned that I was playing football in my condition. He suggested that I stop as he was concerned about my health.

If anyone knows me, you know that I cannot give up even if a probability shows low prospects of success. Could you imagine if Moses refused to go to Pharaoh and be a vessel of God to help free several million people?

Isaac was blind. Jacob limped. Samson was born with a limp and died blind. None of these disabilities hindered these people from testifying to God's goodness. We are all less than perfect yet still chosen.

I graduated high school with a 1.62 GPA. I was last in my class. I was voted most likely to fail. Many people spoke negatively over me even though God had called me for so much more. It was challenging to break out of the mindset that had been molded around me.

I remember during my middle school years "friends" of mine would stain my clothes with a permanent marker. They would add marks and mock me for the number of times I would wear the same clothes to school. I felt embarrassed. I was humiliated. I was rejected.

Relational Rejection

Much of what is considered normal in relationships is really ongoing trauma being rebirthed. Unless you choose to confront your trauma of rejection, it will rule your life.

This is what I experienced as I entered relationships. I wanted to be loved and give love. I did so the best way I knew how. I remember experiencing my first breakup and being trapped in the space of not feeling good enough. I felt betrayed, neglected, and disrespected.

To some degree, it mirrored how I felt towards my father. All I did with purity in my love and intentions was never enough. I never knew my identity and who I wanted Aaron Shawn Harper to be. Each relationship I entered began to define me, leaving me void and empty when it ended.

Rejection in College Football

Years before playing in the NFL, I encountered many struggles in football. I don't think anyone believed I could play professionally.

I did receive an offer to play at a junior college in Mason City, Iowa. I was certainly not smart enough or talented enough in football for a scholarship. I took a leap of faith and took a loan to fund my studies.

My college roommate was a friend of mine from back home. Despite the familiarity of having someone from home with me at college, I was homesick. I felt isolated, like I did not fit in with anyone. Loneliness consumed me. I did poorly during my first year, and I wanted to quit.

Not too long after this, a romantic heartbreak happened. It was a painful experience. I was failing academically and relationally when I had hoped that I would encounter victory.

College was an opportunity for me to step outside of my comfortable environment and grow. What would quitting do at this level? I took a short break then returned to Iowa with a heavy heart.

I ultimately experienced a shift in my heart and mind which was divinely orchestrated. I chose to pursue success, regardless of who would stick by me. I was determined to do better and to be better.

I chose to win despite the hand of cards dealt to me. I had a massive shift in my perception of my weaknesses; I chose to see them as strengths instead.

Rejection Being Shifted to Victory

In my second year in junior college, I tried football again so that I could try to get into a major university. I chose to have a winning mindset and train for the success I wanted.

The cornfields in Mason City heated up to 90 degrees in the summer with no wind, but I showed up and trained. I trained twice a day while taking summer classes. I internalized success and started to see a shift in my abilities. I conditioned my body and mind to get where I needed for football. I took 22 credit hours with night classes in one semester in order to graduate a little earlier and be ready for any opportunities.

Winners are willing to do what others aren't. Yes, I started at a disadvantage, but why would I use that as justification to live a mediocre life when I was destined to do so much more?

I sent out over 200 letters applying to major colleges and universities. I had to borrow money for the postage stamps. I wouldn't hear back from many places, but later I made a name worth being heard.

I realized then that success was possible and that God qualifies whom He calls. God had never called me a failure when I was flunking tests or being cut from teams and kicked out of schools because God never intended for me to fail.

So, how did I become a winner?

I recognized that I could have victory by implementing winning strategies. Using the right principles and heeding the right universal laws leads to a winning life.

Discipline

"Stay focused. Your start does not determine how you're going to finish." — Herm Edwards, Head Coach, New York Jets (2001-05), Kansas City Chiefs (2006-08)

We all have desires, but when it comes down to discipline, your will has to be greater than the pain you will endure to get there. I don't like going to the gym but I know that the reward of health and endurance is far greater than the temporary discomfort I will experience.

I could have remained an average football player who never made it to the league or dropped out of college when I was visibly struggling. The thing that set me apart from those who were in the same boat as me was my unwillingness to accept failure. This wasn't who I was or where I intended to stay.

Discipline can be defined as training created to establish the desired mindset and behavioral habits.

In this simple understanding of discipline I see three key factors:

1. Training

2. Mindset

3. Habits

Take a minute to reflect on an area of your life in which you feel stuck or stagnant and consider:

Are you training yourself in the habits that you want to establish?
Are you conscious of the habits that you want to create?

Pastor Craig Groeschel, head pastor of Life Church, once mentioned *"Our life is always moving in the direction of our strongest thoughts. Most of life's battles are won or lost in the mind."*

What is your mind focused on? Where your mind is focused is where you will be anchored. I had to realize what I was anchored to before I could change my sails to get me to the destination I had in mind.

I had to understand that I was the only person in control of my conduct, despite destructive words being thrown at me. I had to determine that my actions would be the reason for my success.

I knew I wanted to graduate earlier, so I took the night classes. I knew that I wanted to be the best football player that I could be, so I trained harder and focused on nutrition.

I had to decide: Do I complain about the disadvantages I had in life, or do I work with what I have and use it as a motivating factor?

My goal was to increase my self-confidence and redefine myself using the truth of my history. I had to decide how I wanted Aaron Shawn Harper to live and to be remembered.

Discipline is connected to five traits:

1. Ambition. A disciplined person acknowledges their desire to pursue and achieve something and focuses on that determination to reach success. Before I achieved success, I envisioned it. I thought like a winner before holding any trophy. I attained many of my goals through acknowledgment and initiative.

2. Self-assurance. I realized quickly in life that no one would support me the way that I needed them to, so I became confident in my ability and character without relying on others to fill my ego. Assertiveness is a great belief in oneself; when you know you can do it, you will be disciplined to reach your goals.

3. Consistency. I like to think of discipline and consistency as two sides of the same coin. Without consistency, you will not have the discipline to continue your tasks. When I became more consistent, I had more control over my attitude and behavior. I was able to set limits and enforce rules in my life to obtain the goals I set.

It also helped me become more aware of what things were essential and which were not. I began feeling relief as I withdrew my attention from too many areas and focused on a critical few.

Through consistent training, I grew in endurance and perseverance. The amount of endurance I had on day one of training paled in comparison to that of day one hundred.

4. Setting healthy boundaries. Every healthy adult has personal boundaries. Many of us feel drained trying to fill various roles or tasks for others because we subconsciously agree to fulfill them out of people-pleasing. When you set boundaries, you are respecting yourself.

There were many times that I had to reject invitations to college parties because I had to study or wake up early the next day for training. If I had said yes to all those invitations, I'd be running on empty.

A difficult pill to swallow is that others will only respect your boundaries to the extent that you enforce them. This does not mean that you have to be unkind to those who invite you to events, but it means not budging if it interferes with your goal.

Failing to enforce your boundaries breaks the habit of consistency. Boundaries are a part of self-care for personal relationships and emotional well-being. I would rather be well-rested with a healthy set of emotions than have poor boundaries and chaos flooding into every area of my life.

College helped me set the boundaries that served as a foundation for my adulthood. I would not be as successful in the multiple roles I fill now if I had not set up those fences.

5. Focus. Focus is the cornerstone for productive performance. The outcome of your efforts is based on how focused you are. Track runners always hear, "Do not look behind you," while running. Doing so would distract their focus. They need to be running their own best race despite others competing against them.

Discipline set the pace for my success.

I remembered how I would be drenched in sweat with aching muscles which were begging me to stop. Then I would take a breath and realize that if I persevered for another ten minutes, it would eventually get easier.

Every day, my muscles would scream at me in the harsh sun, but I pushed myself further each time. My body would soon be able to exercise for an additional ten minutes without becoming fatigued.

Every day is an opportunity to do better than the previous.

When my alarm would go off in the morning, I would have to choose to see the day before me as an opportunity for greatness. I had to remind myself that soon I would be amazed at what I had accomplished. There is an 80/20 rule that says 80% of the results we see will come from 20% of our activities.

Yes, there were times when I would backslide from consistency and discipline. Getting back to it is ultimately a mindset that must be learned and cultivated with regular practice. Now it comes to me as second nature, just like any other skill.

Napoleon Hill studied a few of the wealthiest people in America for twenty-two years and remarked that their success was due to starting with a clear and significant purpose. Over the years, my ideas of success have changed dramatically. Previously, success meant leaving poverty behind and having money to burn. Now I see success as a measure of how many lives I get to impact.

I can work seamlessly towards my goal of reaching and teaching others because I know the "why" of my life. This is what gets me out of bed in the morning.

While preparing for seminars or meetings, I visualize how revolutionary it will be, and I imagine the impact I will make. I constantly envision my life victorious and then direct my efforts, focus, and habits to accommodate this.

The most important part of a disciplined life is maintaining healthy thoughts. Prov. 23:7 says, *"As a man thinketh in his heart, so is he."*

Our minds carry power. The same mind that can choose to be positive and full of life is the same mind that can decide to end life in a tragic way.

I keep motivational quotes throughout my house as a constant reminder of my journey to overcome unhealthy ways of thinking. I make sure to speak these powerful affirmations out loud daily to reprogram my thinking.

A few ways that I keep good mental health is by staying connected in community and fellowship. I enjoy doing ministry, which is the cornerstone of all my efforts, so I build relationships that allow me to be involved in specific communities and circles of my choosing.

Balance in life is important. Maintaining some degree of fitness or exercise with good nutrition and sufficient sleep also blesses your body and facilitates well-being. It reduces stress and significantly impacts your cognitive thinking abilities.

However, the most significant factor in my life of self-discipline is the Lord. My walk with Him keeps me rooted in a fruit-bearing mindset focused on serving others. Once you have these foundational things in place, it is impossible to keep success from blooming.

In a speech, John Wooden, an American basketball coach and player noted that the top of his pyramid for success is faith and patience. Here is another great quote by a former coach:

"Success isn't measured by money or power or social rank. Success is measured by your discipline and inner peace." — Mike Ditka, Head Coach, Chicago Bears (1982-92), New Orleans Saints (1997-99)

We see athletes like LeBron James, Michael Jordan, and Michael Phelps, who all achieved great success in their professional careers. However, success is a relative concept. If success is measured in monetary value only, it will produce very little joy.

I see myself as successful in the ministry to which God has called me. I find it both an honor and privilege to serve and impact others. By doing so, I am successful in the call on my life. Consider this: if what you are doing currently paid you absolutely nothing, would you think of yourself as successful?

Different, not incompetent.
I knew that I wanted to leave a mark on this earth - even if that meant impacting one life. So I worked harder and I trained longer. I had to constantly decide not to complain or make excuses but to try and shift my plan to match the wins I anticipated.

I never relied on my past wins, however. Things could change at any time. There is no guarantee that you will win a game or be first in your class, but you have to train like it regardless.

Throughout my journey to becoming the best version of myself, I learned the art of not trying to be like anyone else. God made Aaron Shawn Harper to be Aaron Shawn Harper.

No two individuals on the teams I played for had the exact same end goals. We all had our own visions of where our destinations should be.

Think of this: when you're on an airplane, everyone flies from point A to point B in the same aircraft regardless of the destination. Once landed, everyone splits and heads to their unique destinations. The same can be seen in life.

I had to learn to be the best that I could be for me--not what others said I was or what challenges were trying to stop me from getting where I wanted to be. I had to concern myself with what I had control over.

I could control how much I trained and studied. While doing both, the strategies I had in place were always set up with winning in mind. Despite what happened on the field or in the classroom, I knew I did my best.

I had faith in myself, even when the odds were against me. I knew that my God who created me, did so envisioning my success. Whether I had plenty of money or none, I was made to finish the race and so were you.

Often, I see stagnant individuals filled with so much passion and drive to do well in life but have not set up training to achieve the win. Although I was not the best NFL player ever to exist, I did my best to listen to my coach to get better. My consistent results led me to success, and I enjoyed several wins along the way.

Wooden says, *"Success is peace of mind, which directly results from self-satisfaction in knowing you did your best to become the best you are capable of becoming."*

I find myself successful in my relationships with family, the companies I own and run, and with each person involved. At the end of each day I am left thinking, "Am I serving, loving, and doing my best?" If so, I am successful.

Winning Strategies

"You fail all the time, but you aren't a failure until you start blaming someone else." — Bum Phillips, Head Coach, Houston Oilers (1975-80), New Orleans Saints (1981-85)

I speak about mindset a lot because some of us are anchored to ideas of ourselves that are entirely untrue, so we remain average individuals when we are really called to greatness.

As a boy, I do not think winning crossed my mind. In grade school, all I could focus on was making it to the next level. My heart was so heavy and filled with rejection that I could not even see myself as a winner.

Many of my friends and peers received football accolades in high school while I received a mere participation award. I wanted to do better. I had to do better. I was the only person who could decide my fate, and I wanted to look back and see my life as a success, regardless of my struggles.

I don't view my struggles with learning, with my parents, or with poverty as an excuse, nor do I see them as a boulder. I am grateful for what I endured throughout my life because it formed me into the person I am today.

I chose to use what could have tied me down to be the wind in my sails. It pushed me in the direction I needed to go.

The actual turnaround happened in college. When I was faced with many difficulties in my private and academic life, I only had one option, and that was to win.

I knew that the biggest factors in my success would be: my mindset, my will, my discipline, and the training I was willing to put in. After acknowledging what issues could hinder me, I implemented strategies that would help me avoid or overcome those issues, and I continued this throughout life.

I am Aaron Shawn Harper, and I had to align what works best for me within my means. I had to use my own creativity and not the copy-and-paste methods that I saw others using.

Often, when we see a low probability of success, we quit. The probability of me going to a large college and playing football was small. I think many people doubted my ability, but it did not matter what others thought. What mattered was that I was willing to do anything with what I had.

Albert Einstein is a classic example. He suffered from speech delays, which would be considered part of the autism spectrum now. He was seen as a failure throughout his childhood, but as we all have come to know, in reality, he was brilliant.

He also had many setbacks with much of his early work. He tried to rectify his work on special relativity no less than seven times throughout his life. Each time, it seemed that his study was flawed.

Einstein had set the foundation though, and a mere six years later, Max von Laue made a critical advancement in the idea of kinetic energy. This led us to an understanding of today's total relativistic energy.

Sometimes the way we encounter success is not in our wins but by persevering through our failures. Through Einstein's "failures", another individual built on an idea and created a fundamental scientific discovery.

I did not have to be the best football player or at the top of my class, but I did have to try my best so that those who came after me could see my tenacity and be encouraged to succeed in their chosen area. If the idea of failure scared me more than the possibility of success, I used that fear as my motivator.

The following are some winning strategies that I used to move ahead in life:

Create urgency.

College degree programs have a graduation target date of two to four years. This is clearly defined. Knowing what you will do afterwards motivates you and sets a pace for you to implement your career plans.

While I was in college, I knew that I had to earn my diploma, but my mind was focused on what was to come. When athletes are running a race, as much as they are focused on their breathing, pace, and stride, they are all focused on the winning line before them. So, while it is essential to focus on the now, the end goal always has to be in mind.

Outlast the pressure.

The only difference between a successful and unsuccessful person is tenacity. Each day we are provided with opportunities to be the best version of ourselves. You can choose to be complacent and waste the season you're in, or you can decide to be better and push toward the following season.

The Word of God says that we are to rejoice despite trials *(1 Pet. 1:6)*, take courage, and overcome as He did *(John 16:33)* because pressure produces character *(Rom. 5:4)* and endurance *(Jas. 1:3)*, so we should consider it joyful when encountering trials *(Jas 1:2)*.

I have mentioned that I came from poverty, a broken family home, and a history of bullying. Even so, success was never impossible for me, nor is it for you.

I had to work much harder to "catch up" to many of my peers who had an easier life, but I was never dissatisfied with having to work hard. As a successful businessman now, I am grateful for the sacrifices I made in my youth and early adulthood, as they set a place for consistency and tenacity.

When my coach kicked me off the team, I rejected the dismissal. It was an opportunity for me to advocate for myself and prove to my coach that I was able and willing to put in the training to become better. I saw football as an obstacle and an opportunity for me to overcome adversity. Every area of my life was an opportunity for growth.

As children, we all experienced growing pains and they hurt, but it was part of the process of growing. There is no way to circumvent this. When I started seeing my obstacles as opportunities, I started growing.

I have never been able to quit, regardless of how challenging life became. It fueled me to do better. I just had to do better.

I wanted to show others that I could do it. I used the unkind words spoken over me as the motivation and drive to be tenacious.

Whenever someone asks me what the secret sauce to my success is, I say "deciding not to give up". When faced with adversity, I decide to use it as a growing experience.

Our entire reality is built upon how we perceive ourselves, which flows over into relationships, teams, and corporations. When you have self-confidence, you become unstoppable.

You cannot abort pressure, so decide to see it as something positive. Something is brewing that will add to your testimony. There is no such thing as luck, only hard work and favor from the Lord.

Be a life-long learner.

It is prideful to think that you know it all concerning your industry. There is always room to grow. I am constantly learning from my employees, families, and others I encounter. If my heart was closed to learning new things, I would have missed many significant and life changing viewpoints.

After every strategic implementation, I write down what was challenging and how I can circumvent it in the future. Every difficult experience is filled with learning which can facilitate success.

In college, we are not given tests on the first day of class. We have to undergo a process of learning, assessing, and completing projects to grapple with the facts and theories before application. Once we have learned sufficient content, then we test the learning.

It's the same in life. You have to test what you learned and learn what you intend to test.

Learn by failing.

I am more impressed by individuals in my organization who fail and learn than those who experience countless wins automatically. There is much more learned in failure than in success. When we learn to ride a bicycle, we fall multiple times, but we end up riding seamlessly by getting up and trying it again.

Let's take a look at these statistics:

The average millionaire becomes bankrupt 3.5 times.

Seventy percent of wealthy families lose generational wealth by the second generation.

In America, 1,700 individuals become millionaires daily.

Millionaires learn how to manage their wealth. Despite having some hurdles, they are in the process of learning and through their failures, they attain success.

Many of the hardships we endure are simply consequences of failing to plan, refusing to take the advice of qualified individuals, or neglecting responsibility.

Regardless of the amount of failures we have experienced, we can choose to keep learning, keep growing, and keep trying. Eventually, the mistakes will fade and the successes will shine!

Be consistent throughout.

In football, one of the first lessons I learned was consistency. We won many games, but we also lost many games. Regardless of the outcome, we trained and practiced like winners. Our morale stayed high because we were learning how to reduce or prevent future failures in the areas where we made errors.

You become more confident in your ability when you adjust your training. Subsequently, you become much better in your abilities by improving your efforts.

I have found that consistency allows me to know when I am doing something correctly or not. This applies to both my professional career and personal life.

When I would become lethargic during training, I realized that I was not putting enough effort toward endurance and that I should remedy this going forward. When I began feeling bitter, I would work on my relationship with God and ensure that I walked in forgiveness with each person.

If my team's morale is down, I look at how to encourage them. If there is a lack in my team, there is a lack in my leadership.

Assess your environment.
What is in your garden--seeds or weeds? The environment that I was brought up in cultivated a lot of weeds. A hard pill to swallow is that although I didn't sow those weeds in my garden, I was still responsible for uprooting them.

I wanted to blame my father for my rejection and my low self-esteem. I had to uproot the seeds of his words from my garden and replace them with words that would bear good fruit.

I am hyper-aware of what I let into my life, my circle, and my environment. I choose not to be in an environment that is not conducive to my growth. I want to bear fruit, so I have to ensure that every environment I am in helps me cultivate this.

Protecting my environment has allowed me to grow and thrive. I had to place boundaries and learn what I could tolerate and what I could not. We all must take inventory of what is in our garden, whether we planted it or not, and we maintain its health by removing what is harmful.

Surround yourself with people you want to become.
Pastor Craig Groeschel, when teaching Prov. 13:20, mentions, *"Show me your friends and I'll show you your future."* Who you put in your boat will determine whether it sinks or floats.

There will always be people more knowledgeable than you and individuals who are less knowledgeable than you. Who we associate with plays a foundational role in who we become.

Having a mentor and being a mentor are two ways to help yourself and others in this aspect of life. We are to gain knowledge from some and impart knowledge to others.

We usually become friends with others based on commonalities. You must give to friends (in time, energy, advice, and so on) but also receive from them (personal development, encouragement, new experiences).

I would never take advice from someone who isn't walking down a path I want to walk down. I had to ensure that whoever sat at my table was willing to give me valuable advice and build networks with me.

I wanted to be around people pushing me to be the best version of myself, not pushing me away from everything I had worked so hard to achieve. I needed to level up, and only a specific group of individuals would be able to get me there.

Mentorship has provided me with an opportunity to self reflect, share experiences and assess the outcomes of both my personal and professional lives. Finding a good team who provides honest communication, strategic thinking, and effective problem-solving is crucial.

Be willing to adapt to change quickly.
Adaptability is crucial as it expands your capacity to receive change. Individuals who are not flexible often undergo a great deal of pressure and stress when things shift.

I learned to adapt and thrive in most situations. In the plans you make, plan for change!

To develop my skills in adaptability, I had to:

• Improve my creative problem-solving skills in case plans falls through and a contingency is needed on the spot.

• Learn to embrace uncertainty. The COVID-19 pandemic showed us how much we need to be able to adapt to change in every aspect of our lives.

• Push myself out of my comfort zone. Remaining comfortable and playing it safe never grows any team or individual.

• Be open to learning from others to better understand myself.

• Practice self-awareness in various situations to learn how to respond appropriately.

We have limited control over many aspects of our lives, but what we do control is the ability to adapt to change and adopt new ways of thinking. We must choose to follow strategies that complement our lifestyle, position, and environment.

The Success Model
"If you sit back and spend too much time feeling good about what you did in the past, you're going to come up short next time." — Bill Belichick, Head Coach, New England Patriots (2000–present)

In the NFL, coaches are responsible for calculating, creating, and initiating game plans. Without continuously tweaking plans to match possibilities ahead, teams won't be able to confront their hurdles. Apart from pre-game preparation, a lot of analysis is spent in the postgame session.

Postgame analysis is essential to fix plays that did not work out on the field. Coaches gather opinions from the staff and establish better game plans to utilize when the time is right.

This is part of the success model in football. It is also the success model in life. God does not call you to just be successful but to win. God did not call you by image but by identity.

Many people are unhappy because they are trying to attain success without a winning mentality. They are missing their true calling because it does not look like success in their eyes.

For example, some have been gifted with the ability to write, but because it is a complex industry to penetrate, they don't even bother trying. It doesn't seem like a winning move to make.

They go on to pursue other elaborate careers that do not fulfill God's purpose for their lives. I always wanted to be successful, but I had to be obedient to the call in my life.

John the Baptist pointed everyone to Jesus, but was seemingly unsuccessful in his mission because he ended up being beheaded *(Matt. 14:1-12)*. He lived in a way that the world may have despised, but when God looked at him, He saw John as a good and faithful servant.

John lived according to his purpose and was unashamed to walk in what God had called him. Even in his death, he fully lived out his assigned success model.

What is your success model?

Before I could walk into the vision for my life, I had to be willing to be pruned and disciplined to thrive in the success model for which I was created. From a spiritual perspective, I understood that I was created on purpose for a purpose. Many fail to see that there is more grace, blessing, and provision when you follow what you were called to do.

When God placed Adam in the Garden of Eden, He provided him with both purpose (tending to the garden) and provision (food and shelter). All that was required of Adam was to be obedient and perform what God had given to him.

In *1 Pet. 2:9-10,* we understand that we have been set apart to declare Him who brought us out of darkness to His wonderful light as a part of His kingdom. The foundation of a successful model is to understand identity as being part of your purpose.

One can be driven by a sense of monetary reward or fame as a means of success, but as Kendall Bronk (2012) says, "*While seeking fame and fortune may imbue one's life with meaning, doing so does not provide a source of purpose.*"

What is identity?

"We can spend our lives letting the world tell us who we are. Sane or insane. Saints or sex addicts. Heroes or victims. Letting history tell us how good or bad we are – letting our past decide our future. Or we can decide for ourselves. And maybe it's our job to invent something better." — Chuck Palahniuk.

In psychology, identity is known to be an individual's sense or idea of self. It is a set of physical, psychological, and interpersonal characteristics specific to the individual. Identity is determined by morals, beliefs, personality traits, appearance, and expressions of a person or group.

Many of us understand our collective identity in terms of culture or family, but self-identity is seemingly less important. However, your identity drives everything.

When you are conscious of your identity, you reinforce your character. This is because you can understand yourself and your strengths and set boundaries that will work best for you.

When it comes to the issue of identity, much of what we do or don't do is directly rooted in how we see ourselves. How we see ourselves will be reflected in our relationships and our ambitions. When we are secure in our identity, we can make decisions that benefit us and protect us.

We can get lost as we become defined by what we have (or lack) instead of who we are--the innermost version of ourselves. We advertise ourselves by our education, careers, relational status, and parenthood. But underneath all those things, who are you?

I sat with this question for a long time. I had to begin the process of unlearning what others taught me to believe about myself.

God created each of us for a particular reason. God sees us as:

- Made in His image - *Gen. 1:27*
- Chosen and set apart - *1 Pet. 2:9*
- Filled with hope and a future - *Jer. 29:11*
- Individual members of one body - *1 Cor. 12:27*
- Conquerors - *Rom. 8:37*
- Fearfully and wonderfully made - *Psa. 139:14*

Understanding the Creator sets a foundation for understanding self since He is the One Who created us. The fear of God is the beginning of wisdom- *Prov. 9:10*

Why is identity essential to know?

Identity establishes our beliefs. You can think of paper as your identity and the pen you use to write with as the beliefs you hold. Without the paper, you won't be able to see your beliefs.

Every decision that I made was a result of my identity. When I chose to be in football, much of my backbone was created in the sport. I learned many vital skills that formed a foundation for my life and identity.

Having a sense of who you are makes it easier to make decisions. When you know yourself and your identity, you are less likely to be afraid when it's time to make difficult choices.

When I became secure in my identity and knew who I was, accepting certain offers and making decisions was much more comfortable, as I was confident in my choices. Your identity will always be a cornerstone in your journey of winning.

What is your purpose?

What do you intend to see reflected when the rolling credits close in your life? What is the end objective of all of this? After years of attending educational institutions, internships, and training programs, what is your real purpose?

Many of today's youth along with forty million American adults are depressed and being affected by mental illness. This is around one in four adults. They are lost in life and don't know what to do about it.

There is constant pressure to run life as a sprint and not as a marathon. Young adults are ill-equipped for their race, taking off without proper training and resources but hoping to make it to the finish line.

As children, we are constantly asked, "What do you want to be when you're older?" Most of our responses are things we never pursue or achieve. Perhaps this is due to insecurity in our abilities or a distorted view of the future once we're older.

As a child, we were fearless and believed we could do anything. As we became adults, our decisions were tempered and curtailed by forces we didn't realize were working against us to hide our purpose.

In psychology, purpose is defined as an intention to achieve an objective, whether long or short-term, that is filled with meaning and ultimately leaves a positive impression on others or the world. When purpose is unknown or goals are not directed to achieve a result, life can become redundant and meaningless. Purpose is rooted in hope.

What are you hoping for?
I hoped to complete college, to become the best athlete I could be, and to have a stable relationship with my parents. All of these, through effort and discipline, came into being.

"Those who have a 'why' to live, can bear almost any 'how.'" - *Friedrich Nietzsche*

To become successful, regardless of my field, I had to understand my purpose. I had to be set on achieving something that meant a great deal to me as an individual.

After that, I had to involve myself in activities that would allow these achievements to manifest. The combination of intention and activity created a means for my purpose to be established and for it to be achieved.

What is your why? What are you doing to achieve it?

Understanding Yourself

"I've observed that if individuals who prevail in a highly competitive environment have any one thing in common besides success, it is failure—and their ability to overcome it." — Bill Walsh, Head Coach, San Francisco 49ers (1979-88)

I explained the issue of identity when trying to establish a success model. You can also define identity as an intersection of goals, vision, purpose, and self.

The maxim to "know thyself" came from an Ancient Greek aphorism inscribed in the Temple of Delphi. This maxim is premised around becoming aware of our limitations while still understanding what we can achieve. Socrates believed that we could have insight into our human nature by knowing ourselves better.

We have all heard that we cannot change what we do not confront. By doing self-introspection, we can find answers to our character flaws and how we respond to certain things.

Andrea Samadi, the host of *Neuroscience Meets Social and Emotional Learning*, suggests that when we decide to make a conscious effort to know ourselves, it creates a platform to heal and build ourselves up with courage and self-esteem.

We must be comfortable with and accepting of who we are. I have grown to realize that in life, you are either content with fitting in (for the sake of popularity), or you are fine with not fitting.

Some of the most respected billionaires, such as Elon Musk and Jeff Bezos, care little about being part of the most prominent society. Instead, using their purpose, they create and invent new platforms that will benefit everyone.

Could you imagine if either Musk or Bezos had to ask an expert's opinion about something only to have it rejected and torn apart? As the faces of Tesla and Amazon, do you think they would take that as their identity and see a business plan failure as an identity failure? I don't think so.

To be successful, you have to know yourself well. Musk mentioned in an interview that much of his time is spent at work despite having plenty of time for leisure and rest. Because he constantly has new ideas, he has to make space to weigh and assess the feasibility of a project before starting it.

I had to take a step back when I was older and think about who I wanted to become. I was not "finding myself" but taking an inventory of what I had and working with that. God had placed inside of me gifts and talents that he intended for me to use and grow into. All I had to do was work with what I had.

If you're reading this and you're on the journey of finding yourself, I want you to consider what traits, history, connections, visions, and goals you already have.

I used to think of poverty as a curse but came to realize it was an opportunity. As I explained, my father left when I was younger, and my mother became the breadwinner. My mother cleaned homes for wealthy people and those beautiful homes made me want to live a better life.

I wanted to stand out and rise up. Unfortunately, in grade school, we are taught a conformity mindset. We are taught to think the same, dress the same, and graduate as good employees. There is little room for innovation, creativity, or a pioneering mindset ready to blaze new trails.

School was established to create workers. We spend years in educational systems to graduate and then be herded like cattle to help those at the top build *their* dreams. As children, we are taught to be critical of others for being different, yet as adults, we celebrate it.

I was created to be radical up to a point, and we should dare to be different. All tremendous scientific developments happened by going places no one had ever gone before, trying things no one else would try, and believing what no one dared to believe.

To go against the grain and do something that no one has ever done is not easy, but it is worth it. Winners have to decide to run that race despite the possibility of losing. This is ultimately what distinguishes winners from losers: they no longer follow a path of comfort but choose to lead.

I had to be willing to change my mindset and be uncomfortable with mediocrity. I trained myself in a manner to see myself as my only competition. No one else starts the race on your line, nor does anyone run at the exact same pace.

God's calling on our life will not be encountered if you are swimming in the shallows. There is nothing more powerful than understanding that God is for you and that you have the authority to establish who He has called you to be.

"Your work is to discover your world and then with all your heart give yourself to it." — Buddha.

I was willing to answer the call because I was conscious of myself and where I wanted to go. The process of knowing who you are takes discipline. You have to be willing to push past hurt to embrace the healthiest version of yourself. You have to see yourself from a fresh perspective, free from the opinions of others that cloud your judgment.

By knowing my strengths and weaknesses, I have found clarity on what contributes to and hinders my growth as an individual. I had to dive deep into my natural abilities while working on those that did not come like second nature.

Many will know you by who you present yourself to be, but you are the only person who knows the true version of yourself. This is the person you must chase after.

You have to develop a way of programming yourself to continuously grow in areas that you feel are your strengths. Work on your skills and talents and look at ways to capitalize on them.

Are you naturally gifted at music, sports, math, or teaching? Have a look at educational programs that can advance your skills or consider making a career that is heavily dependent on those talents or skills.

There will always be fluctuations in particular interests and hobbies, but the ones you find yourself going back to might be the core of who you are.

Are you more right-brained in the creative, emotional, visionary, or entertainment realms? Are you more left-brained in the analytical, detailed, logical, or critical-thinking ways of doing things?

Nothing thrives more in a winning environment than an authentic individual. You have to be relevant to the environment that you intend to impact. You can begin to see your self-identity as:

- Beliefs
- Emotions
- Interests
- Dreams
- Talents
- Principles
- Goals
- Values
- Habits
- Personality

Whether you choose to define your identity by your career, social position, or physical features, ensure that you are rooted and grounded as someone you are proud to be. You can always reconstruct your identity as you grow, but understanding your core beliefs and values is crucial.

As I look back on my life, I see the combination of all my hobbies, social roles, personality traits, and abilities forming part of my identity. I can do well in my career as a motivational speaker because I know precisely what individuals in certain leadership positions need to hear.

I count myself blessed to be able to impart, equip, build, and train individuals and teams to become the best versions of themselves. I recognize that everything I endured and went through in my life was building up to this moment—the moment to engage and empower the next generation of leaders.

Understanding Hindrances

"When you are willing to replace mundane excuses with hard work and your laziness with determination, nothing can prevent you from succeeding."— Dr Prem Jagyasi

Everything is possible to overcome.

Regardless of who you are and where you come from, there will be hurdles to overcome. We are responsible for how we perceive our hurdles.

Based on my upbringing, success was far-fetched for me. It did not mean that it was unattainable but that it would require a lot more from me.

When it comes to hindrances, you have to assess and evaluate what could hold you back from reaching your destination. This is entirely different for each person.

Some people are born with a silver spoon in their mouth but still never achieve the things they intended. In contrast, there are many people born below the poverty line who use their hardships as a springboard to go for their dreams.

What is preventing you from becoming the person you envision? Is it your mindset or lack of resources? What can you do with your present means to help you get to the next level?

If you look up the definition for hindrance, it is described as something that causes "resistance," "delay," or "obstruction." None of these need to be physical but can be any impediment experienced during the developmental stage.

Growing up, I saw my financial position and learning disabilities as physical and mental hindrances to my success. Eventually, both proved to be crucial factors in my success.

A few of the most significant obstacles, according to a popular blog named Entrepreneur, include:

- Time
- Lack of focus
- Holding back
- Attitude
- Fear

As you can see, most of what hinders us from achieving success is in our minds. Let's discuss these now...

Time Management

Every individual is afforded the same 24 hours each day, and what you decide to do with them is entirely up to you. You must choose in advance to be efficient with your time. When you can manage time well, you will experience greater productivity.

Some enjoy the rush of working under pressure as a factor of motivation. This might work for a little while, but it will not be effective in the long run.

When you plan ahead what you will be doing with your time, you are less likely to become distracted. You will then be able to accomplish more high-quality tasks in a shorter period of time.

As a businessman, husband, father, sibling, and friend, I must ensure that none of my roles are neglected. I started to plan my time according to priority. What requires immediate attention? What steps do I need to accomplish my goal, and how much time will it take? Based on my answers, I set up my schedule accordingly.

"A billion seconds is just over 31 years. The 20-year-old has two billion seconds (left). The 50-year-old may have one billion seconds (left). Take a step back today and ask yourself — do I invest my capital based on the greatest resources I have access to?" Anthony Pompliano of The Pomp Letter.

Graham Duncan coined the theory titled "Time Billionaire," which was based on the principle of living a billion seconds. He remarks that if you do not expect to live until then, you should aim to be a "time millionaire".

Many of us encounter the fragility of time just when it appears to be running out. Time is the most valuable asset on this earth.

You do not have to obtain your bachelor's degree by age twenty-four or be married by thirty. How you choose to spend your time depends on you and how you define your needs and desired achievements.

Of course, I struggle with time management occasionally, but I have a team that supports, encourages, and reminds me. This is part of winning for me--having structure, support, and strategy in place to assist me in getting to the next level.

There is no single billionaire, millionaire, or CEO who does not have an assistant. This plays a foundational role in time management. Having productivity apps on your phone or mobile device or even an accountability partner also helps to protect your time.

Once you start to see time as a finite asset that has to be protected, the more willing you will be to win with every second. Your age means little, but how you choose to use your time means everything. Some individuals have only lived twenty or thirty years but have lived complete, whole, and purpose-filled lives.

As Alan Watts says, *"(It's) better to have a short life that is full of what you like doing than a long life spent in a miserable way. And after all, if you do really like what you're doing, it doesn't matter what it is, you can eventually turn it-- you could eventually become a master of it."*

Lack of Focus

In 1991, Bill Gates, Sr. had an exclusive dinner party with his son and Warren Buffett. During the dinner, Gates, Sr. posed a question asking what others considered the most important factor that resulted in their success or current position in life. Buffett immediately retorted by saying, *"Focus."*

Despite being an immensely successful and focused individual, Buffett still has time for hobbies, including the card game, "Bridge". His interest in the game demanded a lot of focus and dedication to become a master at it.

He later entered a world bridge championship with two-time winner Sharon Osberg. While playing, onlookers noted that he appeared to be transfixed in the game and it seemed as if he was completely ignoring his surroundings. It was like he was the only person in the room.

Buffet qualified and went through to the final round of the competition, despite it being his first tournament. He worked tirelessly to compete in that final round, but he pulled out at the last minute due to fatigue.

Many might remark that this was not a winning mindset. I beg to differ. To work hard and focus your efforts on achieving something whether you compete or not, or win or not, is winning in itself. The race is against yourself and no one else.

Steve Jobs commented, *"People think focus means saying 'yes' to what you've got to focus on. But that's not what it means at all. It means saying 'no' to the hundred other good ideas that there are. You have to pick carefully. I'm as proud of the things we haven't done as the things we have done."*

When you are conscious of your purpose and all that you wish to fulfill, you will be able to prioritize and remain focused on the tasks at hand. Most professional athletes, musicians, actors, or business people owe their success to their focus, not their talent or ability.

Holding Back

A hard pill to swallow is that sometimes, we are our own worst enemy; our thoughts anchor us down. A psychological term, known as "self-handicapping," is a cognitive strategy people use to avoid effort(s) that have the possibility of hurt or failure.

There are two types of self-handicapping. The first is *"behavioral handicaps"*, rooted in actively self-sabotaging or creating obstacles to performance, projects, and achievements. This can be seen in athletes who fail to show up at practice leading up to a game because they are already expecting to lose.

The second is *"claimed handicaps,"* which are fabricated hurdles put up by an individual who anticipates loss or failure. So, they willingly speak, claim, or accept what they think could materialize, such as a sickness or injury.

Assess what barriers are holding you back. Common ones are:
- Envy
- Perfectionism
- Comparison
- Blaming
- Self-doubt
- Fear
- Distraction
- Unwillingness to step outside your comfort zone

Regardless of age, I always tell people to chase after what they are passionate about. So what if you fail? Get back up and try again. It does not matter how many times you find yourself down; what matters is how many times you are willing to get up, push through, and go for it again.

I promise you-you will regret more the things you didn't do or never tried instead of the things you did try, even if you failed.

Attitude

"If you want to make a permanent change, stop focusing on the size of your problems and start focusing on the size of you!" — T. Harv Eker, Secrets of the Millionaire Mind: Mastering the Inner Game of Wealth.

Attitude can be defined as how you think or feel about something. It sets the foundation for how you perceive the world. Your attitude consists of emotions, beliefs, and behaviors toward a particular object, person, or event.

A great deal of your success is based on attitude. Psychologists perceive and understand attitudes as a learned tendency to evaluate things in a particular way. There are three components of attitude, namely:

- **Cognitive:** thoughts and beliefs about a subject matter.
- **Affective:** how a particular subject matter makes you feel.
- **Behavioral:** how your attitude influences what you do.

If these components do not align with each other, it causes internal instability. You need to understand how you truly perceive and feel about certain things. You can change your attitude to align your behavior to a more favorable outcome.

Attitudes are formed through:

- Experience
- Social factors
- Learning
- Conditioning
- Observation

Attitude is crucial in determining how you will cope with the affairs of daily life. You will be more willing to remain disciplined if your attitude is fixed on the correct things. Your attitude is always a choice.

In the NFL, it does not matter what reputation the opposing team has, you still have to train and direct your efforts to win. A negative attitude in one player can ruin the entire team.

It takes a tiny piece of mold to ruin a fruit, so imagine what a negative attitude can do to your success story. I had to decide, regardless of my feelings, to attend training sessions and perform at my best.

Fear

"Failure defeats losers, failure inspires winners." - Robert T. Kiyosaki

Success anxiety is a real thing. We consider the possibility of achieving something but disregard it for a plethora of perceived threats, most of which will never occur.

At points in my life, I was the only person preventing me from my success. Yes, the odds were stacked against me and I was scared that I would ruin my opportunities. These thoughts made me consider quitting.

There was a growing concern in my mind that I would never reach my potential. However, a small and insecure voice in my head asked, "But what if it works out?"

Fear of succeeding is by no means rooted in inability. Fear is planted by words and experiences as seeds in our hearts.

Sometimes we value someone's opinion so much that when they disregard our ambition, it deters us from pursuing it. Therefore, growing up, I developed "imposter syndrome". This is where I thought I was incompetent or inadequate even though there was evidence to the contrary.

I had experienced so much rejection, isolation, and bullying that I thought I would become the negative words that people called me. This could have held me back from the life I was meant for, but instead I used it as fuel to take me to the next level.

Everything you desire to achieve stands at the door of trying. Whether you win or lose at first, lifelong learning occurs when you can circumvent the same errors in the future.

You have to take inventory of the fears you have. You are responsible for using the opportunities and resources available to you. Some other symptoms of the fear of success include:

- Seeing all criticism as an attack on your character and skills
- Discomfort with trying new things
- Rejecting change
- Losing support networks

Once you're able to understand your fear triggers, you can work to introduce strategies to help you overcome them. You can do this by visiting a life coach or therapist or talking to someone who has been in a similar situation.

Furthermore, it is essential to remove any negative influences that will make you question yourself. The company you keep plays a massive role in your life. Some people are comfortable having you at a certain level and will try to hold you from sailing off to success.

Start implementing healthy boundaries with those who drain your energy or will. When I was focused on improving my training and grades, I had to say "No," more than I ever had in my life. This allowed me to focus on my journey and grow the core abilities that launched me into the future I was desiring.

In a speech by Morgan Freeman, he mentions that following your dreams involves the magic of risking everything for a dream that nobody sees but you. Regardless of how small your steps might be, if you are moving forward, it means continuous improvement.

I do not know who you are, but I am a living testimony of God's strength and wisdom despite where I came from. The destination you are moving toward is far greater than the minor hindrances you are experiencing.

Do not stop because you have a hindrance, but use that as a platform to kick off. I am rooting for you because I know you can do it!

Walking Through Forgiveness

"Words without action fall on deaf ears." - Aaron Rodgers, Future Hall of Fame Quarterback, Green Bay Packers (2005-present)

If you knew that today would be your last, would you be content with the way in which you concluded your last conversation with each person who was part of your life?

A difficult thing for many to understand is that forgiveness is more *for you* than it is for the person you are forgiving. Walking around with a heart filled with unforgiveness is like hiking up a mountain with a bag full of heavy rocks and expecting it not to weigh you down.

You did not get to decide what trauma you experienced, but when working towards healing and spiritual growth, you get to decide to release what was a burden to you. To move towards the future, you must make peace with the past. If not, you will continue to live in the past and die in the present.

Unforgiveness impacts more than your ability to have healthy relationships; it significantly impacts your overall well being. "There is an enormous physical burden to being hurt and disappointed," says Karen Swartz, M.D., Mood Disorders Adult Consultation Clinic director at The Johns Hopkins Hospital.

According to Hopkins Medicine, unforgiveness impacts your blood pressure and immune response, which increases mental illnesses such as anxiety and depression. It also increases the risk of heart disease and diabetes.

Forgiveness is more than a mental response to someone. It is premised on an active decision to remove any negative feelings that are harnessed toward someone, whether you think they deserve hostility or not. Eventually, you will be in a space where you can hold empathy and understanding for the person you worked towards forgiving.

Unforgiveness can impact generations to come. If you consider your family structure, you can at least think of one person who is considered the "black sheep" or who has not spoken to or been involved in family gatherings for some time. The hostility between a few people is now being passed down to the children, who absorb those negative social interactions and behaviors.

While trying to establish my future, I could not be handcuffed to the past. One of the best things we can do as healing and growing individuals is to recognize that every person is a product of their pain. This does not justify abuse, ill- treatment, or any such actions that may have been placed on you, but it builds an understanding that you were never the problem.

No one wins in a culture of unforgiveness. It contributes to a weak character in the unforgiving person, not the person who is the source of the offense. An Australian army nurse coined a popular statement, *"He who angers you, conquers you."*

While you are not required to forget the hardship you endured, forgiveness is a mechanism to circumvent dwelling on the past while protecting and allowing yourself to move on. There is strength in deciding that despite the wrongdoings, regardless of who is at fault, you will forgive them. You can hold people accountable for their actions or words, but forgiveness releases their power over you.

It is crucial not to minimize your suffering, but equally, not to see it as a beacon to spread hatred. You cannot alter the past, but you can decide not to suffer and hold on to the pain for the rest of your life.

You are not necessarily required to reconcile with the one who hurt you. Once you achieve the emotional space from healing, you can decide what is best for you. This is not based on feelings but on a rational basis of what is good for your well-being.

Col. 3:15 says, *"Let the peace of Christ rule in your hearts, since as members of one body you were called to peace. And be thankful."*

Fighting through bitterness is key. When I worked through unforgiveness, particularly with my parents, I had to remind myself of its importance. I did not want to forgive them just so that I could go ahead and live my life. I wanted to understand them and deal with how I felt in those moments.

As I mentioned, my father leaving was a life-changing event in our household. It was heartbreaking, but I knew that if he had stayed, it would have destroyed me. He had to leave so that I could grow. When my mother urged me to play football, once again my life changed completely as I learned many skills and grew my character significantly.

When it came to moving forward in my faith, I knew what I needed to do. I had to shift from anger to forgiveness. I recognized that if everyone saw me as who I was at age ten for the rest of my life and did not allow me to rectify wrongdoings or to grow and improve my character, it would be an awful life.

I knew that I had changed because I allowed my mind to rebrand my father and shift away from the past. I allowed myself to move forward with love for my father.

"The best revenge is massive success." — *said Frank Sinatra.*

I realized that unforgiveness was hindering my healing when I finally understood my underlying motivation to achieve success. My desire to become successful was really built on the foundation of proving my worth. I had built a "them against me" mentality that was premised on showing others that I could do it.

To many, this might not seem like an awful motivation, but it is an unhealed perspective of winning. I wanted my success to be built on a new version of myself that was healed. I wanted to win in life because it was *my* desire and not the expectations of others being held over me.

It takes a lot of maturity to understand that all your wins in life are for no one else but you. You have to be proud of yourself when your efforts result in real achievements.

I recognized I needed to change my motivation because:

- It was laced with ego.
- Unforgiveness and anger always destroy the container it is held in.
- When you try to prove others wrong, you show that you believe what they are saying about you.

Recognize that forgiveness is not a one-time event but a continuous decision to love individuals who hurt you. You cannot win with bitterness. Furthermore, forgiveness looks different for each person.

I focused on being willing and able to listen while being slow to anger in certain conversations with my parents. It was crucial to me to have boundaries in place to protect both my heart and theirs. This avoided a great deal of conflict.

By removing a fixation on the past and deciding to see the best in my parents and others, I removed hostility from my heart. God called us to love others as He loved us first.

We have seen in the COVID-19 pandemic that time is fragile. Avoiding things until you are comfortable enough to have certain conversations is not the best. Nothing is promised, regardless of how healthy we might be right now. The only time that exists now is the present. Aiming to live a life filled with forgiveness and grace allows us to better embody Christ to others.

Of course, there were times when I slid back into my emotions, but I gave myself the same grace that I extended to others. Forgiveness is a process that takes time and determination. I have to continuously be gentle with myself and allow myself to be human.

By God's grace, I can heal the emotional wounds inflicted by others. I understand that those who hurt me, even though their actions and conduct were never justifiable, are all humans who require grace to be extended.

We are always given the opportunity to decide what to do with the hurt. Part of healing is realizing that you were never the problem and that the decision is always yours to rise from the ashes or succumb to it.

Which will you choose?

Living a Life Filled with Gratitude

"When I became the head coach, I said that we would ask you to come in and give everything you had every day. And you did. I am so proud of you, grateful for you, and I believe in you." - Joe Judge, New York Giants Coach (2020-2021) and New England Patriots Offensive Assistant (2022- present)

As I reflected on my journey up until this point and considered what else enabled me to create a winning lifestyle, I recognized the impact of gratitude on my journey.

I love the definition of gratitude, which is "a quality of being thankful" or "readiness to show appreciation." I came from humble beginnings, so as I grew to be more financially secure and have a steadfast reputation, gratitude came to me as second nature.

"Cultivate the habit of being grateful for every good thing that comes to you and to give thanks continuously. And because all things have contributed to your advancement, you should include all things in your gratitude."- Ralph Waldo Emerson.

My mother taught me how to be thankful for all that I had. I was always in awe of my mother. Regardless of how much we had, she always thanked God, reminding me of our source.

In every situation we found ourselves in as a family, my mother would encourage us to pray and give thanks unto God. This is something that I still practice. I am thankful each day that I wake, for every talk I host, and every meeting I run.

I can relish in new experiences because I see nothing as random or coincidence but everything as a blessing. God calls us to be thankful, and we can see that in several scriptures, such as:

- *I will give thanks to the Lord because of his righteousness; I will sing the praises of the name of the Lord Most High. - Psa. 7:17*

- *I will give thanks to you, Lord, with all my heart; I will tell of all your wonderful deeds. - Psa. 9:1*

- *I will praise God's name in song and glorify him with thanksgiving. - Psa. 69:30*

- *Do not be anxious about anything, but in every situation, by prayer and petition, with thanksgiving, present your requests to God. And the peace of God, which transcends all understanding, will guard your hearts and your minds in Christ Jesus. - Phil. 4:6-7*

- *So then, just as you received Christ Jesus as Lord, continue to live your lives in him, rooted and built up in him, strengthened in the faith as you were taught, and overflowing with thankfulness. - Col. 2:6-7*

I start from a place of gratitude. Many wait to see an outcome before deciding to express thanks in their lives, but I have found several benefits in my well-being, relationships, and overall relationship with God by expressing gratitude even when I experience adversity or changes.

First, I acknowledge Him as the source of all goodness. There is no one good but God alone. We all receive many blessings in life and they all come from Him. I make an effort to thank God, not only for what He has already done but for what He is going to do.

Secondly, I make sure to recognize the good that does come into my life. This can be in terms of ministry or speaking opportunities to which I am invited, the people in my life now and those I will meet, and the many resources I've been given.

We can miss out on many things if we are focused on what we do not have, instead of all that we do. We might be thankful for some seasons in life more than others, but there is always something for which to show gratitude.

In a psychology study conducted by McCullough, Emma, and Tsang in 2002, they found that individuals who practice gratitude daily grow strength as a character trait.

Offering gratitude in life assists with:

• Better well-being as more focus is given to the positive aspects of life instead of what is lacking.

• Interpersonal relationships that are strengthened with the bonds of mutual respect, value, and trust.

• An increased sense of happiness.

• Greater discipline, as self-control is used in making better choices which reduces destructive behavior.

At the University of California, Professor Ye Li mentions in a study, "... *a simple gratitude exercise opens up tremendous possibilities for reducing a wide range of societal ills from impulse buying and insufficient saving to obesity and smoking.*"

I am thankful for many things, including being able to serve my community. I remember thinking back then how amazing it would be to impact my community and offer them resources I wished I'd had.

After talks or seminars, I leave better than I came. I am thankful for all the lives that intersect with mine, regardless of the duration. There is not a single person I have met who has not impacted my perspective or life.

Here are some simple ways to express gratitude:

• Journal your thoughts and give thanks for the blessings.

• Verbalize your appreciation to friends and family.

• Perform random acts of kindness.

• Include others in your plans, especially those who are going through a difficult time or are lonely.

• Listen intently. Regardless of the role you occupy, listening with understanding and not merely responding does more than you think.

• Volunteer or offer a donation to a non-profit organization that matches your values.

Whatever you feel the Lord prompting you to do in terms of expressing gratitude, just do it!

I pray that you choose to live out the life you envision, give without expectations, and extend forgiveness to everyone. If you do these things, you are a winner!

You are capable and you have what it takes! With God all things are possible! Achieve the victories that you have always dreamed of and go WIN!